Nick Marickovich

Application
for the
Apocalypse

...And Other Poems

Wider Perspective Publishing ¤ Hampton Roads, Va. ¤ 2022

Copyright © April 2022, Nicholas Marickovich
Wider Perspectives Publishing, Norfolk, Va
ISBN: 978-1-952773-53-2

To Mars and Rosalyn,
and to all who have inspired me, past and present.

contents

State of Mind, August 2017

I feel at times that I am just the sum
of those things I have consumed:

Anti-depressants and vitamin D mixed with
coffee to keep ill humors in check;
Food to fuel the machine,
grinding grist for the new Rome:

The power coursing through my laptop,
Kindle, iPhone, wrested from a vengeful earth;
The fair trade shirts and cloth grocery bags
that allow me to tell myself I still give a shit,
tell myself that one can still make a difference,
shrugging off a thousand inconvenient truths;

Mozart Violin Concertos to make me feel
wealthy and privileged as I drive to the store,
not because of the color of my skin and
the luck of the draw but because of the
content of my character, my cultural efficacy,
the bootstraps I keep hidden in the glove box;

So many books on war that when I think
about my life I see soldiers fighting in
wars long lost, skillfully withdrawing
back to some point at which all things
simply implode into nothingness.

The car I have driven into the ground like
a knackered horse;

Before I turn the key
in the fitful ignition I reach my left
hand up towards my throat, fingers
searching for the thin chain with it's
gold cross that my mother gave me,
blessed by an Eastern Orthodox priest
from Cleveland that I will never meet,
flinging holy water in a warehouse full of crosses
ranged in rows like those on dormant battlefields,

lost souls running into the steel teeth of life,
proof that I haven't given up just yet.

Not Writing

Could I be happy not writing?
Putting the pen away for good?

I'm not quite sure what I would do.

Perhaps eat pierogies till I die;
Sit and watch one generation
lapse and fade into the next;
Churn out war machines to support
my daughters' future dreams,
which I hope turn out to be
so much loftier than mine.
Scroll through the shattered shards of Truth,
rubble of the nation written
in tweets and memes and You Tube posts.

I'd hunker down, get comfortable,
live a life as pointless and as
fragile as a soap bubble
caught in a breeze.
What else can any man do
as water heats up slowly,
insidiously, 'til it boils?

Yet flowing through my inner depth
there's this aching desire to
scratch immortal words into the fencepost:
"I was here!"

In which Nick Actually Completes a Poetry Challenge

It was asked, by someone much more thoughtful than me,
"What is it you plan to do with your one wild and precious life?"

I plan to write lousy poems about having dinner with
Alexander the Great, Winston Churchill,
Napoleon Bonaparte, and Võ Nguyên Giáp
At the Hooters in Guam,
Outpost of American Democracy in a vast, unconquerable sea,
Purveyor of the finest teriyaki-garlic wings I have ever tasted.

Dinner does not go as planned.
Alexander is entranced by the concept of a fork;
Churchill fumes over the restaurant's no-smoking policy;
Bonaparte ogles waitresses, believes he has somehow turned up
In a sort of delightfully tacky yet unrefined Valhalla;
Giáp keeps pushing his last mozzarella sticks
From one side of the plate to the other,
Running out the clock on this
Disastrous dinner date.

But then my eye catches something:
Risk, the game of world domination,
Sitting improbably, miraculously,
In this den of timid titillation,
A thick layer of dust on the top of box.
I set it up on the table, explain the rules.

I can see Alexander eyeing
The green expanse of Asia,
Churchill rubbing his hands, overcome
With gleeful anticipation of recapturing
Empires lost,
Giáp mulling a fortress Australia strategy,
Siam the bait, the deathtrap,
Springboard to ultimate victory.
And Napoleon, dear Napoleon,
He wants it all, you can see it in his eyes,
Little blue plastic soldiers
Conquering the entire globe
Pour la gloire de la France.

I order another beer. This evening just got interesting.

That is what I will do with this one wild and precious life.

Equal and Opposite

I don't believe that I have a soulmate.
Instead, I think I have an equal and opposite reaction,
Spinning counterclockwise through space and time
While I spin clockwise, mathematically perfect.

I think I saw her once, dancing during a Ska set
At an outdoor concert, dreadlocks down to her waist,
Nose stud glimmering in stadium lights,
Body flowing like water under a claret skirt
And a low-necked sweater.

I stood and watched her for a long moment,
Steeped in her magic, not daring to approach,
Lest our destinies crash into each other,
Exploding in a tragic supernova and
Undoing the balance of the Universe that
God so carefully placed
On the edge of a knife.

Jean Reno

In my dream, French Actor
and Mission Impossible star Jean Reno
and I are sitting in a pastoral forest,
eating apples and brie with folding
knives that cost a fortune:
Damascus steel, titanium frame,
blades etched with Monet Paisley.

He asks "Why are you not
enjoying the brie?" and I tell him
that I want to leave my book club
because I am not enjoying it,
all we read is postmodern
novels with point of view shifts
that are supposed to take you
into the wellspring of life,
but when you get there
it turns out most people
are a closed fist whose primal
concern is simply to fuck,
and make money
so they can fuck some more.

Jean Reno eats a piece
of cheese and leans back against
a log, says that he knows
personally the cow whose milk
made this brie. Her name is
Mathilde, and she enjoys it
when someone scratches behind

her ears, and her milk is best
when someone reads her
Moliere at night.
I wait for, then search for,
the meaning or the metaphor
behind his words but find nothing.
So I go on.

I tell him there is this woman in the
book club who I am dying to know,
and I worry that if I leave I'll never
see her again. But at the same time,
I know that whatever might
exist between us will be
awkward, unfulfilled,
unconsummated, unbearable.

And Jean Reno turns to me and says
"Did it ever occur to you that maybe
you are the reason that she is still
in your miserable club? And that
the only reason another person goes
is because she is there? That your
entire book club, and maybe the
entire universe, is being held
together by nothing more than
your quiet yearning
for this woman? That without
it, all things would dissolve
into a mathematically
unresolvable chaos, and

we'd go spinning hopelessly
into the cold void of space forever?"

Then Jean Reno cuts an apple slice
and winks, the signal to the sniper
hiding on the hillside to engage,
and as the bullet streams towards me
the entire universe collapses
into a black hole of desire and doubt
in an infinite millisecond.

I wake up to sunlight
filtering in through the blinds.

Eucharist

As we nibble on Christ's Body
And sip his Blood from small plastic cups
The organist plays music matching reverent moods.

I know she's bored, she keeps tossing
Musical jokes into the midst of her meditations,
Today she takes the Doors' "Soul Kitchen",
Manzerak's opening gambit,
Stirs and strains it
Through a melancholy Mahler,
Easy to hear if you know what to listen for.
Lithe, bluesy rock and roll
Shifting sensuously under layers of dour
Grey music, heavy like
Coarse Victorian clothing.

As I kneel for the host she gives me a wink,
Today's joke is meant for me,
Reminding me of when we
Stood in her kitchen drinking wine
On a hot summer afternoon. She leaned
Against the counter, raising the
Large glass up to her lips,
Smoke from her cigarette curling back
On itself as it floated out the window
Up towards heaven,
A prayer of Thanks.

Eating Beignets Teleported
from New Orleans

A new day begins slowly descending the stairs to the kitchen,
Time worn knees creaking and groaning.
At the table my son sits with fresh beignets
Made minutes ago in New Orleans,
Teleported to our local Fulfilment Center,
Delivered by one of a thousand drones
Latticing the skies with boxes and bags
Clutched in mechanical talons,
Bringing "it" to the consumer in the blink of an eye,
Whatever it is, whatever you want,
Whenever you want it.

He pairs them today with coffee fresh from Paris
From some little café where artists and philosophers
Used to meditate on unanswerable questions of life,
Where girls of society high and low
Smoked bad French cigarettes, and played their
Coquettish games with art and skill, their bodies the prize,
Guarded jealously by a fortress of
Cloth and clasps, corsets and buckles;
But also with a propriety and patience dusted lightly
Over their souls like the sugar coating these beignets,
Not overpowering yet somehow inviting, delightful.

He lazily proclaims these are the best beignets you can get.
Maybe he's right; but I don't enjoy them as much as when
His mom and I drove down to New Orleans before he was born,
Trying to get to a wedding for people we didn't like.
Ten hours of consulting maps and arguing over exits,
Wandering in the low country like wayward paratroopers
Probing cautiously in the darkness,
Praying for a sign that we were close,
A sign we must have missed; we arrived three hours late,
Surrendered at a beignet stand in the city.
We wolfed them down hot out of the fryer,
Fortified ourselves with bitter coffee
So thick you could stand a knife in it.
She looked at me across the table with those eyes,
Those eyes of deep green, irises flecked with gold.
She took my hand. We walked together into a city
Bursting with music and light.

To Albert Camus

I'm retiring my black turtleneck,
setting it on fire and burying the ashes
outside the café where I once
fancied myself a philosopher,
smoking cigarettes and staring
into space with bemusement,
half empty apricot cocktail on the table,
chin resting on the hand just so.

I cannot do it, Albert.
I cannot live with a haughty defiance,
fiddling away on the knife edge
of Kierkegaard's ledge,
spitting in the face of life's
meaninglessness with every
labored breath spent
creating, conquering, loving;
soldiering on with like minded
comrades though the hour grows late,
the noose slowly tightening
toward our inevitable fate.

So Bold! So Heroic! But I'm not
strong enough to live that life,
I find no solace between the
cool legs of a French Algerian beauty,
nor any consolation in the mere dignity
of stoically straining to
push the boulder up a muddy slope

only to watch it roll down the hill again,
leaving me laughing at the absurdity
of my predicament, of my life.

No Albert. I cannot live this way.
I need my heart to be lifted up,
I need my sins to be washed away,
I need to shine in the light of Glory.
I need to take the easy way out,
and leap off the ledge
into the waiting arms of God,
my own personal Lord and Savior,
my own little Plastic Jesus.

A Poem About my
Eighth Grade Algebra Teacher

She was a dry stick of a woman,
Looking at the class with large green eyes
Set in huge window-frame glasses,
So long unfashionable,
Through which we tasted the wrath
Of her uncompromising zeal for math.
Partial credit is for the weak, she says,
Something reserved for English class,
Which may as well be basket weaving.
She strolls among our desk and repeats
Her fanatical mantra that

if
           a sign is missed
           a decimal is displaced
           a unit doesn't work out

then
           the bridge falls down
           the ship sinks
           the brave astronauts of Apollo 11
                 burn up and die in re-entry.

It's hard to imagine her kicking back
in silk pajamas with a glass of red wine,
hard to imagine her in love,

hard to imagine that maybe once
someone snuck into the teacher's lounge
and left a slip of paper next to her
breakfast of bitter tea and burnt toast,
containing not words but equations,
describing how she had set a heart aflame
with unquenchable desire, that a
soul was in danger of falling apart
by the unrequited feelings twisting
its psyche into resonance.

Did she, maybe, see a missed sign
or a displaced decimal in this declaration?

Did the units not work out?

Did the brave astronauts of Apollo 11
burn-up and die in re-entry?

An Engineer Makes Pancakes

We sit at the kitchen table, waiting.
The engineer weighs his ingredients carefully on a properly
calibrated scale,
Muttering as he adds flour pinch by painstaking pinch,

Seeking exactly one hundred and thirty point zero zero grams;
Removes a little flour here
      at one hundred thirty point four five grams,
Adds a little there
      at one hundred twenty-nine point eight seven grams,
Takes some away, adds it back in again, tacking ever closer
To the exact amount that will combine seamlessly
With other painstakingly measured ingredients to yield
Pancakes of precision, pancakes of perfection,
Pancakes of scientific exactitude designed to set the neurons
Ablaze with pleasure at approximately
One hundred eighteen point eight seven two meters per second.

We sit at the kitchen table, waiting still.
We flip through a book of paintings by Jackson Pollock,
Souls hungry for art, stomachs howling
      for a little bold, shambolic beauty.

While Loop

n = 1

    while n = 1

        if d = Monday

            Go to work;

            Chit chat about uneventful weekend;

            Drink horrible coffee;

            Save Shipyard;

        end   %Go Home;

        if d = Tuesday

            Go to gym;

            Go to yoga;

            Take shower at gym;

            Wonder about rules regarding direct

                proportionality of shameless nakedness

                in locker room to age;

            Go to work;

            Fight for parking spot with the blue Nissan;

            Cover self in the glory of valiant defeat;

            Park one mile away;

            Drink horrible coffee;

            Save Shipyard;

        end   %Go Home;

        if d = Wednesday

            Go to work;

            Drink horrible coffee;

            Laugh wearily over two-year-old hump day joke,

                the one where one camel asks the other

                camel what day it is;

            Laugh though the light in your eyes is dull;

            Save the Shipyard;

```
end       %Go Home;
If d = Thursday
          Go to gym;
          Go to yoga;
          if headstand = 1
                    chance of tryst with yoga instructor =
                              chance of tryst with yoga
                              instructor + 0.000125;
          else
                    chance of tryst with yoga instructor =
                              chance of tryst with yoga
                              instructor – 0.001;
          end
          Take shower at gym;
          Go to work;
          Fight for parking spot with the Blue Nissan;
          Emerge victorious, salute enemy for gallantry;
          Drink horrible coffee;
          Bring Shipyard to its knees;
end       %Go Home;
if d = Friday
          Go to work;
          Drink horrible coffee;
          Recommend changes to coffee making procedures;
          Get met with deaf ears;
          Leave work early;
          Go to bar;
          Contemplate getting tattoo;
          If beers consumed > 12
                    Get tattoo of garish Matisse nude
                              on lower arm;
                    Call her Petunia, make her dance;
                    Vomit in the street;
```

19

```
                        else
                        end %Go Home;
                end
        if d = Saturday or Sunday
                        Open Moleskine Journal;
                        Flip past exhortation that this
                                was the journal of Van Gogh,
                                Picasso,
                                Hemingway,
                                Chatwin
                                and turn to blank page;
                        Wonder again who Chatwin is;
                        Pour scotch;
                        Stare wistfully out window
                                with hand resting on cheek
                                just so;
                        Be a poet;
                        End up writing nothing;
                end
        L = RAND(0,100)
        if L < 99.99977
                        n = 1 %Better luck next week!
                else
                        n = 0 %Ah, life, my dear fellow: 'tis but a shadow
                                and a dream.
                end
end
```

The Cat Looks Out
an Open Door

I told you it was raining,
but you didn't believe me.
You had to see for yourself,
sticking your head out the open door,
sniffing the heavy, humid spring air.

I leave the door open for you, for a while.
Freedom beckons just over the sill,
everything you ever wanted;
the thrill of the hunt,
tall grass to stalk through,
nature's hard, sublime artfulness,
out there, waiting, for you.

You don't put a paw forward,
happy to live in the warm, boring familiar.
Still, you stand there, looking out
beyond the sill for a long, long time,
miming your consideration,
showing me that its your choice,
that you have the power,
that you hold all the cards,
even though we both know,
as the door is closed,
that it isn't true.

Donut Day

Wednesday is donut day.
Will I have one, you ask?

Well, you see, donuts are my enemy.
They raise cholesterol, expand the waist,
Grease up the fingers and pimple the face.

But sadness, true, is my enemy too,
Clouding souls with depressing density,
Robbing life of beauty and pleasantry.

Cannot donuts, with sugar, carb, and fat
Send neurons into sacred resonance,
Banish darkness, bring some blessedness?

That would make donuts the enemy of sadness.

The enemy of the enemy is my friend.

Please pass the donuts.

Santa's Christmas List

What would I like for Christmas? Well well, let me think.
First and foremost I'd like a new drink.
Milk's so blasé and it gets so darn warm.
It'd be nice if cold beer was the norm.
Cookies are good, but sammies are too,
And crackers with brie, or maybe beef stew.

What else, what else, let me dig through my thoughts.
Sometimes my brain gets all tied up in knots.
I'd like a computer to keep track of lists,
My elves are arthritic, their hands give them fits.
Their handwriting's poor, they write so darn small.
Sometimes...I wish I'd no helpers at all.
But it's a big operation, it's got to be done!
...What I'd like most of all is to just have some fun.

Maybe retire and go see the sights,
Take Mrs. Claus out for eight crazy nights.
Slowly sip coffee in Paris Cafés,
Jump on a Harley and drive far away.

Humbug! What rubbish! I've got all I need,
To want anything more's gratuitous greed.
My noble task is to spread Christmas Cheer,
It makes my heart glow for the rest of the year.
And trust me, dear friends, that will suffice,
Though between you me, a beer would really, really be nice.

Honor

– or A Poem I Wrote After
Watching *The Queen's Gambit*

Things start to wear after
half an hour, conversation
growing stale while our coffee
grows cold.

I get the sense she is the kind of person
who would hold up Dee Dee Ramone
as some kind of musical genius,

A thesis I not only
disagree with but violently
object to. I have no way
of knowing this,

yet I know somehow, it's true;
worse, I know she knows I know.
She begins to look for
an elegant way out,

A wily chess player
puzzling over a position,
looking to avoid a
desperate, inevitable,
sloppy endgame.

At last she finds it, says
she is sorry, she really must be going.
I finish an almost undrinkable latte
and resist an urge

to leap over the table and
kiss her out of sheer joy
for letting us retire with
Full honors from the field,

flags flying, bands playing,
a little brass cannon dragged through
the mud behind, signaling
willingness to fight on another day

just with somebody else.

The Girl at
the Sportsclips

In Newport News, on a Tuesday,
the girl at the Sportsclips,
with the brown hair and metallic pink clippers,
gives me the best haircut I have ever received.
It's the kind of haircut you build a life upon,
something marking the passing of one epoch
into another, of darkness into light,
one solid point on which to carefully construct
the scaffolding for something new, balancing carefully
a host of new expectations, desires, demands
now orbiting around this altered sense of self,
something that is me but somehow also better than me,
a billion lush possibilities blossoming into life.

Six weeks later, on a different Tuesday,
the girl at the Sportsclips,
with the brown hair and metallic pink clippers,
gives me the worst haircut I have ever received.
It's the kind of haircut that tears the rickety façade
of happiness and purpose to the ground,
sets my mental dashboard ablaze like a Christmas Tree
with warning lights and tripped alarms.
Like a jaded test pilot whose seen it all,
I seek a safe place for a crash landing,
schedule an appointment with a therapist,
ask my doctor for a dosage increase,
compulsively buy yoga equipment that might

provide the next point on which to
precariously stand and rebuild,
balancing on a rocky ledge
with hands in prayer pose,
trying not to fall.

Reading Middlemarch

After two months
I'm not even halfway through.

It reminds me of accounts I've read about invading Russia,
how space just keeps expanding out in front of you,
limitless nothingness,
dotted here and there with a village, or a town.
The deeper you drive into it, the more the steppe swallows
you whole, and though you roll through
page after page, line after line,
the church spires of Moscow stay
always over the horizon, smugly out of reach.

As the fall, filled with rain and thick, sticky mud,
is followed by the first winter snow,
you wonder if reading a
study of provincial life in the 1830s
can really make you a better person,
if it can offer relevant insight
to the human condition
that cannot be communicated with
something simpler, more soothing:
a painting, a sculpture,
a comic book, a movie, a binge worthy
series; a golden mug of beer
poured by a waitress with a smile.

Shivering by the Berezina River,
waiting for death or the Cossacks to come
will you chuckle ruefully, and
ask yourself if it was worth it?

That is the question I ask myself,
as I pick up my edition,
a heavy millstone I cannot discard,
and turn to page three hundred and eighty-two,
even though I know, deep down inside,
I'll die before I ever finish this book.

Joltin' Joe

I read once that Joe DiMaggio
smoked a cigarette and drank a cup of
coffee between most innings.

What if he played in our more enlightened age,
and someone bothered to tell him
about the basics of hydration,
and the harmful effect of smoke on the lungs?
But even more, got him a fitness
coach and a personal chef to give him muscles
he never knew existed, turn him into a
finely-tuned machine exquisitely, tenuously balanced,
easily sent into disarray by one errant tweak:

a leg overextended sliding into second,
an awkward landing after robbing a homerun,
an ankle twisted on a pebble in the basepath,
hiding in the white chalk with malicious glee.

Maybe, in that parallel universe, for all the
good advice and intentions wielded in service
to create the ultimate baseball player,
Joltin' Joe is doing another stint in Toledo,
on rehab assignment with the Mudhens,
nursing that bum hamstring and
wistfully wishing for a stiff cup of coffee
and an unfiltered smoke.

Von Kluck's Turn

Schlieffen said the last man on the right
should brush the Channel with his sleeve.

On August 30, 1914 Von Kluck chucks that plan
onto dusty French roads near Lassigny,
orders his columns to slowly wheel south.
The move, he thinks, will end the war
in the perfectly prescribed 39 days.
Instead, he gets a French attack on the flank,
British soldiers marching through gaps in the line,
the smashing Miracle on the Marne,
starting the race for the sea
towards stalemate, trenches, and death.

Years later, while I watch the hurricane churn
through the sea towards the shipyard,
hoping for some pressure ridge to build and
shove it eastward, I think about Von Kluck's Turn.

Dad laughs at me over the phone when I tell him,
says I must be the only person alive who
is reminded of the German First Army
when looking at a hurricane forecast.

I don't think they are that different.

Both are massive things that move slowly, maliciously;
both are forces of savage destruction and desolation;
both remind me of how history is built on
wrong turns, innocuous decisions, changes of course,
the random roll of a dice that brings chaos,
showing all of us that while we dance
we dance on a
very
thin
line.

Truth

Truth is as fleeting as a summer romance,
sweeping you off your feet in a warm embrace
of certainty, making you feel like you matter.
Like you're something.
Like you are a small cog upon which the rest
of the Universe turns about towards
some perfect point in history where there are
cakes and ale for everyone.

But one night sitting together on the couch,
you see Truth is watching the news
with the same wide-eyed disbelief as you,
sipping whiskey with trembling fingers,
a shawl wrapped around slumped shoulders
too narrow to carry Truth's own campaign promises,
let alone your own fear of staring into the depths
and finding only nothingness.

Truth moves in when the leaves start to fall,
but things feel different now. Things are left unsaid,
questions remain suspended in dusty autumn sunlight.
You find the gears of history are not
oiled by dogma but rather rusted with blood,
clicking, groaning to push the rock up hill,
only for the relentless dawn to reveal
that it's rolled back down to the bottom again.

You say that this isn't the way
you thought it would be. Things are supposed
to have meaning. Things are supposed to make sense.
Truth just shrugs, arms crossed over her chest,
asking what exactly you expected from this relationship,
offers you nothing in consolation but a cheesy greeting card
and some cheap gas station wine on the faux marble
countertop in your cold kitchen, marking
the five-month anniversary of the first time you saw her
in that coffee shop popular with the Jesus Freaks,
and were enchanted.

A few weeks later Truth moves on to someone else.
When at last she comes back for the few things left behind:
a toothbrush, a few books,
The Monty Python DVD with the scratch in it,
you realize you share much of the blame for how it turned out.
You demanded too much,
pressed to hard; you let Truth slip
through your fingers like the foggy mist
from which she first emerged.

Jo Van Gogh

I am left with an apartment in Paris,
a few items of furniture,
and rooms full of worthless paintings.
That's all there is.
That's all that's left.

Everything Vincent touched
wilted and died: his friendships,
his whores, his brother. My husband.
All for these unsellable paintings.

Friends say I should throw them out.
I'd love to. I'd love to build a big
bonfire and dance around them, naked
(Ol' Vincent would like that, wouldn't he?)
flinging these canvases into the flames,
rejoicing as I turn them into ashes, one by one.

The idea of being free of them, of him,
shimmers like a mirage
in a desert of despair.
My body aches to the core for the
cool waters of a clean start.

But these paintings.
These worthless paintings.
I'll make people love them,
I'll make their beauty known,
I'll hitch my soul to their popularity,

and to the mystique of that tortured
ass, Vincent Van Gogh.
I'll squeeze something meaningful
out of this pain, this suffering,
this wretched desolation.

Because if I cannot do that,
what else is there?

Reformation, 500 Years On

Five hundred years ago Martin Luther,
suffering from existential despair
and perhaps a bit of indigestion,
nailed 95 Theses outside a
church door in Wittenburg,
changing history.

Not that he meant to.
He didn't want to make so much of a fuss,
like your aunt and uncle from Dixon Lake
don't want to be too imposing,
though they note that the coffee you made
isn't quite black enough,
and the chairs need to be reupholstered,
and Peter the Dog has a
wistful, anguished look in his eyes,
signaling that he might benefit
from some sort of therapy.

I think of your aunt and uncle while
I sit with Peter the Dog in Church,
trying to bolster his spiritual well-being.
I wonder if the Protestant Journey
ends this way, in pancakes
and pretty good poems,
with people cloistered behind walls
leaning on canes bent deep under
the strain of years,

all of us seeking reassurance
that the answers to life's biggest questions
remain unchanged within
very precise dimensions of the Trinity.

Maybe 500 years on someone needs to tack
95 more Theses inside the door.
Deep inside a Mighty Fortress no one sees the sun.
Get out of it once in a while,
be a light in a world of darkness.
Sin boldly, love much,
welcome all who come in peace,
feel the cool grass beneath your naked feet
as you peruse some of those pretty good poems,
while Peter the Dog sits near, still wracked by
existential despair, and maybe a little indigestion,
from sneaking some of those pancakes
out of the garbage.

Triumph

382 days after having begun and
Nine years after the last episode aired,
I finally close the book on The Sopranos.
I feel like I've accomplished something;
86 Episodes, over 4600 minutes of sometimes
Brutal TV, digested like a bad meal from
Nuovo Vesuvio; rich, delicious, upsetting,
Hitting back with bilious acidity,
Leaving one retching with disgust yet
Somehow wanting more all the same.

In ancient days I'd demand a Triumph,
A parade through the streets showing off
Spoils from a long campaign, while
Vestal Virgins toss heaps of gabagool into
Throngs of adoring masses.
There stand statues from Jennifer Melfi's
Office, nudes in German Impressionistic style,
Angular, intimidating, serving as a first warning
That behind the door they guard is a lousy,
Self-centered therapist.
There is the body of Sal Bonpensiero,
The severed head of Ralph Ciffareto,
The ghost of Christopher Moltisanti,
Screaming for our sympathy, asking to
Never mind a life of casual brutality
Cut short deservedly in kind.

And there's me! Sitting in my chariot,
Covered in glory, clad in a well-tailored suit,
Two of many nameless strippers from the Bada Bing
Standing behind me in topless tableau, holding
Wreathes of cigarettes and whisky over my head,
Whispering in my ear over and over again
"You are just a man.
You are just a man.
You are just a man, and you've accomplished nothing."

Launching the
USS WASHINGTON

The first thing you must know is that it was cold.
Rain was falling from a sky colored like the
Bad gas station mocha I bought at 2AM
Before coming into the shipyard.

Maybe that's why I felt like I did,
Standing there on the bow of the
USS WASHINGTON, as the submarine
Snuck off the docking blocks to little fanfare.

In Russia they might bless it with
Church bells or choir music.
In England, some regal lady might
Deign to look down her royal nose at it.

But here, as our newest War Machine
Tastes the brine of brackish water for the first time,
There is nothing but the hum of diesels and
the sound of the James River lapping her steely flanks.

I find myself alone, wondering how I picked
Up five inches of forward trim,
Misgivings trickling down my spine,
Rain pelting against my hardhat,

Like someone's tossing pebbles against
Closed windows, trying urgently
To get my attention
In the middle of the night.

Taco Tuesday

It is Taco Tuesday on a US Navy Nuclear Submarine.

Sitting in their tepid chafing dishes are
not tacos, but rather hard tack burritos
and questionable tamales.
Everyone ahead of me gets one of each.
When it is my turn I inquire,
if it's not too much trouble,
if I could have two burritos.
CS1, by the considerable power vested
in him by the United States Navy
and years of vaunted tradition and majesty,
rules that I may have one burrito and/or
one tamale, but having two burritos,
or two tamales, is simply out of the question,
a most egregious violation of naval protocol
set wholly upon his mighty whim.
One of each, one or the other,
or none.

Well, fuck you, CS1.

I want to lean over the serving line and grab
the whole tub of tamales and burritos,
run up forward and load them into the
countermeasure launcher, shoot them out
into the briny deep one after another
"BLAM BLAM BLAM BLAM BLAM!"

so they all sink to the bottom of the ocean
to be eaten in darkness by those fish with
fucking lightbulbs growing out of their foreheads
so they can see just what it is they are about
to sink their sharp, prehistoric jaws into,
though I wonder if, for them, it really matters.
Food is food, survival is survival.
Burrito, tamale, it doesn't matter.

It doesn't matter. But I still hate tamales.

"I guess I'll have one burrito then", I say aloud,
touch of anger tinging my voice. CS1 places it
on a plate, dry and heavy like a stone,
flash frozen somewhere far ashore
and reheated here under nuclear power,
at 50% Test Depth. It's incredible what we
can do today, dreams undreamed by
warriors of yore, eating a pill full of beans and
beef while sitting in a metal tube,
inches of steel separating life from death.

That burrito, it was magical,
engineered with incredible properties
of a nutritious and gastro-intestinal nature.
I know the CS1 really had my best
interests at heart when he said I
could have only one;
too much magic in the hands
of one man is nothing to be trifled with,
as the crew runs through their drills

of turning keys, destroying cities,
practicing for the day when they
may be called upon to be
vengeful, American Gods.

Belgium v. Japan, 2018 World Cup
– July 2, 2018

In the 68th minute,
with Japan up 2-0,
I feel so very low.

I used to cheer for
plucky underdogs,
those among us who would
thumb their nose at the system,
refuse to conform to convention,
yet somehow win all the same,
who attack with fury and joy,
leaving our more stolid,
conventional selves mystified,
flat footed.

But now?   The history I know
Is not the history you believe in.

In an age of Post Truths,
I seek something solid to stand on,
like I'm just past the breakers,
seeking the sandy bottom
with outstretched toes,
head barely above water,
wondering when the next wave
is going to come.

Tonight I need something to be true,
and that something is that Japan
should not win this game.
Their football is daring, desperate.
The Belgians should be too cool for that,
able to pick through the midfield
in spaces left by Japan's furious
full on heavy metal press,
at times virtually the entire
team going over the half-way line
to regain possession,
dancing dangerously with doom!

But the Belgians are flummoxed;
they see the truth too but it
remains beyond their grasp,
and now the looks on their faces
make you think
they aren't going to make it,
they are going to fail;
as the game enters into
the final phase I feel
myself sinking slowly,
easing into a miasma
of deep depression, as the
fabric of my reality continues
to be undone, stitch by stitch.

When Belgium completes
their comeback with a
blistering counterattack in the

94th minute to win 3-2,
I do not react with joy,
I am simply relieved;
a little bit of order
and comforting predictability,
blooming for a moment in the desert
as we reap the whirlwind,
sown by charlatans peddling
those great American myths
like snake oil off the backs
of the poor.

Application for the Apocalypse

I wish to join your post-apocalyptic
anarcho-syndicalist commune.
I have many useful skills.
Chief among them:

I am very good at picking things up,
moving them a certain distance,
and putting them back down.
Not like a Himalayan Sherpa,
undisputed champions
of carrying things. But...

You should have seen me
in the before-times,
schlepping groceries from the
trunk of my blue Hyundai with the shitty breaks
up to my apartment on the third floor,
two whole flights of stairs,
my body festooned with sacks and plastic bags,
full of frozen eggrolls, Oreo cookies,
various circular meats,
several bottles of fizzy water
Christ I'd let you cut off my left
big toe for a bottle of San Pellegrino,
or even Perrier flavored with a kiss of grapefruit,
the worst kind of fizzy water there was,
reserved for Bourgeoise languishing
in mediocre suburban Purgatory.

Life without fizzy water has no meaning,
at least that is what I used to believe,
before all of this...

My lesser abilities are many, varied.
I can throw an axe a pretty mean distance,
I have very discerning taste
when it comes to cheesecake,
with enough practice I think
I could open a bottle of champagne
with a curved calvary saber.
I can restring the guitars
played by your bands of merry men,
even play a song or two myself,
weave stories together on dark nights
when the moon is hidden,
when twinkling stars are replaced
one after another by the crackling campfires
of your enemies on distant hill sides.

I've felt the pains of loss,
I know what it is to be tossed into the Abyss
and yet keep moving,
always upwards,
until you claw your way out
and learn to love again,
if indeed love can exist
in a world such as this.

Take me on. You won't be disappointed.

Before the Somme

It was a few days before the Big Push.
My two pals and I left battalion,
made our way towards
La Maison de Poulet Vert,
because little Kenny Keegan
from Company E
said if he was to die
he would not die a virgin,
no matter what the cost.
We would bear 'im up, support our lad,
and figured that if little Kenny Keegan
can, then so can we.

We followed him to the door of
La Maison de Poulet Vert
and the madam answered,
ushered us into a seedy parlor,
put glasses of cognac in our hands;
where she got it from I really don't know.
I'd never tasted it before, like fire
in the throat. Little Kenny Keegan
gulped his down and asked for another,
and I figured that if little Kenny Keegan
can, then so can we.

What to do next? We didn't know how
to ask for what we wanted. None of us
spoke the soldier's French that asked
for woman, wine, and song.

I thought with some relief that
our night might be at an early end,
but little Kenny Keegan, not to be deterred,
made the proper hand signals
to communicate our needs.
I gulped in fear, sweat breaking out
across my brow,
and figured that if little Kenny Keegan
can, then so can we.

The madam winked and called the girls,
they floated down rickety stairs
like ghost ships, garish gowns and garters
flying with straps, buckles, lipsticks, ribbons,
lewd smiles striking not desire
but fear into the heart. My knees wobbled.
We stood. Madam's brandy boiled in
my stomach. Earnest faces back home
clouded my field of vision,
wearing looks of sharp disappointment.
I glanced at Dhalglish, I signaled Hodgson.
We bolted, leaving our three pennies
spinning on the table, with little Kenny Keegan
happily ensconced in skin and silk,
being borne up willingly to rooms above.
Little Kenny Keegan could, but
I, apparently, could not.

I saw him again 4 weeks later, wearily
slogging towards the saps while I was trudging back.
His face brightened into a smile, for a second,

and I shook his hand as he passed by.
We were glad to see each other,
both still alive.

At least for now.

Charlie Brown

When Charlie Brown grows up
I think he'll be a professional cyclist.
But not a great one,
not one you would ever remember.
He never learns to ride with no hands, so he's
afraid of crossing the line first
during a stage of the Tour de France;
he is unsure of what he'll do if he
can't lift his hands off the handlebars
and hold them, palms up towards
the sky, in a gesture of victory and thanks.

So, he'll be a domestique,
schlepping water bottles
from the team car to the other riders
while Lucy radios in, screaming
that the breakaway is going to be caught,
it's time to get organized at the front,
it's time to take his place in the line,
it's time to grind it out in high gear
as long as he can,
to lead Linus out in the flat,
to let him draft off Charlie's wake,
to let Linus slingshot out of the
boundary layer created by that
giant, beautiful bald head
for the final sprint to the finish,
victory in all its glory, with the crowd
and the cameras and the pretty girls

who kiss Linus' cheeks in
French fashion while he wraps
himself up in that stupid blanket of his,
threadbare with age, that he can't seem
to let go of despite years of therapy.

Charlie Brown thinks about all of this later
as he gnaws on a stale baguette, while
team busses and cars caravan to Nice
for the next stage, focuses his intention
on riding all the way to Paris,
how it will feel to round that last corner
onto the Champs Elysees,
an experience reserved only for a lucky few.
His mind wanders past the tired brokenness of his body,
he allows himself a moment to daydream
about a post-Tour sojourn in Marbella.

Realizes he simply couldn't be happier.

Watching the Snow Fall,
Oxford

I stand outside the gates of Christ Church College
watching snow fall late on a cold night.

My room across the narrow street
sits in a building supported by timbers
felled hundreds of years ago.
The warped floor lists crazily to the left,
as if the whole building might just give up,
collapse with a wheeze of exhaustion
and dust.

A church bell chimes in a watchful spire.
I wonder how many people have stayed in that
guest room with its slanted floor,
listening for the whispers of ghosts
wandering through the halls,
haunted by unrealized dreams and dashed hopes
that speak so loudly on a dark winter's night
like this, all of them as unique as snowflakes
now falling from the sky.

It should be enough to catch one,
look at it closely.
You could lose yourself in
its mathematical perfection,
its crystalline beauty,
even as it melts in your hand,
turning back into a few drops of water.

The Print of Van Gogh's Cypress Trees Hanging in my Therapist's Office

I ask myself what Van Gogh,
Teeth stained with paint,
Cheeks hollowed by syphilis,
Breath reeking of coffee and liquor,
Lonely, Unhinged, Sour,
Denied by even the cheap whores of Arles
The false joys of purchased pleasure;
What would he say now that
His turbulent trees, skies, grass,
Rendered violently in deep gouges,
Provide cold comfort to the splintered mind?
That from the fractured self
One might yet etch something beautiful
Into the transient night.

Bass Player

There he goes again.

He's the only one in the band
that really, truly, speaks to the audience
beyond a mumbled "Thank you" between songs,
or the relived "Good Night" at show's end.

I wish he wouldn't.
He thinks he's got that perfect punk blend
of quirky and funny, finished with an
iconoclastic sarcasm
dusted over his soul
like confectioners' sugar.
But he doesn't have it.
Worse, he doesn't know it.

He's here because he's a human metronome,
and can remember almost all of our songs;
because his brother bought us beer
when we practiced in his mother's garage.
He's here because
that's what a bass player should be,

the unsexy facilitator
without which none of this is really possible,
not some musical Lenny Bruce
cracking wise like its open mic on two taco Tuesday.

Our fans are good natured,
giddy, high, and laugh at his awful jokes.
No one has the heart to tell him
that truth we all must one day confront:

That none of us are half as charming
as we imagine ourselves to be.

Lying on the Floor in Winter

I lie on the floor in winter. It's cold.
I'm listening to songs by Nirvana
Just as I have since I was twelve years old,
When sadness put on her silk pajamas

And made a nice nest down deep in my soul,
Put up new curtains and stayed for a while.
She turns my thoughts into swirling black holes,
Laughs I struggle for a Roman Mile,
Burdened by her sultry agony,
Heart buckled by bittersweet gravity.

So sometimes this is all that I can do.
Press my face into the floor, let music,
With its healing grace, make my heart anew.
Though I wonder if it's therapeutic,

Weaving dark sonic threads throughout my life,
And if among depression's pointless strife
There is a comfort, after all, in being sad.

Listening to Watershed, by the Foo Fighters, 22 Years Later

The music carries my mind away in a dream,
melds with my body, my soul.
For a moment I still feel
my legs and arms finding that extra gear,
with 200 meters to go,
spiked flats ripping into rubberized track,
racing now, almost flat out but not yet,
for the finish.

The best days of my life? Hardly.
I don't believe in such things.
I see a kid, brave, naïve,
a bit full of himself,
mistaking the cracks in his foundation
for the adversity that makes a man,
intent on acting out his own
part in the great American tragedy
that has been unfurling since its founding,
heady mix of heavy metal and heavy weapons,
ending with a folded flag if necessary,
sanctified with sacrifice – oh yes
there's nothing sweeter than dying
senselessly for someone else's greed,
another name chiseled into the wall for freedom,
and he knows it.

Thank God for the asthma that clouds his lungs
even as he closes in with 100 meters to go;
his dreams may have been consummated
in a dusty hamlet far from home
rather than being simply dashed
against the rocks.

So on to Plan B. The playbook
sticking out his back pocket
prescribes a life that doesn't fit;
setting it aside will be the hardest
thing he has ever had to do,
and its possible he never will
get rid of the albatross of expectations
that hangs about his neck.
If you can't fight for the American Dream
you may as well live it,

even though the wages of sin is debt,

and he'll feel sick to his stomach
when a ship he worked on
pops a couple cruise missiles
at some country we don't really care about,
because some charlatan in a red tie orders it
along with his overdone steak
in the comfort of his private club,
and when he realizes that
every inch of this aircraft carrier is designed

to put ordnance on target,
you can hide the bombs under
Red Cross blankets when
a hurricane rips through some country
most people can't find on a map,
but the truth is they are always there,
ready to go,
ready to rain policy and death
on deserving and undeserving alike.

All done in the name of domestic tranquility:
the house, the kids, the two cars and a cat,
the psycho-sexual no man's land of the marriage bed,
honeymoon duvet bunched into a
Berlin Wall with snipers in the towers,
while beyond the white picket fence
Jesus kneeled and wept and went unheard,
riot police serving tear gas and truncheons
to the oppressed, to the marginalized,
even though they say all lives matter
while they sip chardonnay
and stock up on hollow points.

It'll all fall down.
The more he tries to fix it the more
it just collapses in on itself,
he tries to resurrect something from the ashes
but they get blown away in the wind,
as ashes always have been
and always will be.

The song is almost over now,
and I can see him in a full sprint
down that final stretch.
I want to go back,
not to tell him any of this,
but to let some of my anger
bleed back into him,
it's something he lacks,
the savage joy of leaving
someone in your dust,
of sending them down
in fucking flames.
There should be that much for him,
at least, as he leans into the finish line.

Depression, July 2020

All I want to do is
sit around and eat cheese—
all day.

I know if I want a life
after this life I really shouldn't.

I'm not sleeping well,
drinking more than is healthy.
I know.

I can't seem to finish anything,
everything is left undone.
Half-completed novels,
movies with twenty minutes
left to run,

My own heavy thoughts,
things long left unsaid,
even this poem
which

Dosage Adjustment

They doubled my dosage.
I realize now I had forgotten what happiness feels like,
How to live in the moment,
Enjoy the warmth of sun on skin,
The rippling of rye in gentle winds;
The feeling that God is tapping your shoulder,
Asking you to dig how beautiful it is out here,
And maybe you should say something righteous,
And hopeful for a change.

Unbidden despair still stops by every so often,
Knocking on my door in deep starless night,
Christmas Roses woven in her hair,
Skin latticed with scars.

I show her around the place,
Proudly point out the spackle smoothing
Out the cracks, still a bit wet to the touch.
She peaks into the crawlspaces,
Points out the fatigue in the foundations,
Unresolved questions threatening to
Bring the whole thing down.

She gives me a kiss on the cheek.
She'll always be there for me, she says,
Waiting.

Her time will come. But for now, let her wait.
Right now?

I'm drinking wine,
I'm eating cheese,
I'm catching some rays, you know?
Right now, I simply can't be bothered.

Eighty-Four Cents

I have Eighty-Four cents in my pocket.
Three quarters, a nickel, and four pennies, to be precise.

I hold it all in the palm of my hand, gauge the weight,
Feel metal slip and grind against metal between my fingers,

Marvel at how nothing can really feel like something.

Meet Your Poet

Nick Marickovich grew up in Blacksburg, Virginia and attended Virginia Tech, graduating with a degree in Ocean Engineering in 2005. From June 1 through December 10 of 2005 he hiked the entire Appalachian Trail, 2175 miles, from Maine to Georgia. He moved to Newport News in 2006, and works at Newport News Shipbuilding. He started writing poetry in 2014, and this is his first book.

Colophon

Brought to you by Wider Perspectives Publishing, care of James Wilson, with the mission of advancing the poetry and creative community of Hampton Roads, Virginia.

This page used to have many cute and poetic expressions, but the sheer number of quality artists deserving mention has superseded the need to art. This has become some serious business; please check out how *They art...*

Grey Hues
Madeline Garcia
Chichi Iwuorie
Symay Rhodes
Tanya Cunningham-Jones
      (Scientific Eve)
Terra Leigh
Raymond M. Simmons
Samantha Borders-Shoemaker
Taz Weysweete'
Jade Leonard
Darean Polk
Bobby K.
      (The Poor Man's Poet)
J. Scott Wilson (TEECH!)
Charles Wilson
Gloria Darlene Mann
Neil Spirtas
Jorge Mendez & JT Williams
Sarah Eileen Williams
Stephanie Diana (Noftz)
Shanya – Lady S.
Jason Brown (Drk Mtr)
Ken Sutton
Crickyt J. Expression
Lisa M. Kendrick

Cassandra IsFree
Nich (Nicholis Williams)
Samantha Geovjian Clarke
Natalie Morison-Uzzle
Gus Woodward II
Patsy Bickerstaff
Edith Blake
Jack Cassada
Dezz
Toni Lynn Britton
Catherine TL Hodges
Kent Knowlton
Linda Spence-Howard
Tony Broadway
Zach Crowe
Mark Willoughby
Martina Champion
... and others to come soon.

the Hampton Roads
      Artistic Collective
      (757 Perspectives) &
The Poet's Domain
are all WPP literary journals in cooperation with Scientific Eve or Live Wire Press

Check for those artists on FaceBook, Instagram, the Virginia Poetry Online channel on YouTube, and other social media.

Hampton Roads Artistic Collective is an extension of WPP which strives to simultaneously support worthy causes in Hampton Roads and the local creative artists.

Made in the USA
Columbia, SC
08 May 2022

60028589R10046